(PK20)

C000192831

fresh
in summer

fresh
in summer

RYLAND
PETERS
& SMALL

cooking with Alastair Hendy

photography by David Loftus

First published in Great Britain in 1999
by Ryland Peters & Small
Cavendish House,
51–55 Mortimer Street,
London W1N 7TD

Text © Alastair Hendy 1999
Design and photographs
© Ryland Peters & Small 1999

Printed and bound in China
by Toppan Printing Co.

ISBN 1 900518 86 4

A CIP record for this book is available from the
British Library

Acknowledgements
My thanks to Egg, of Kinnerton Street, Belgravia,
in London, who were so generous in lending
beautiful bowls for photography, and Kara Kara,
of Tokyo and Pond Place, South Kensington in
London, for Japanese ceramics and other props.
Thanks also to Cityherbs of New Spitalfields
Market, London, for their useful information and
high-quality produce, and to Rebecca Hoyes and
Alasdair Parker for lending us their kitchen and
garden for photography.

Notes
All spoon measurements are level unless
specified otherwise.
Ovens should be preheated to the specified
temperature. If using a fan-assisted oven,
cooking times should be reduced according to
the manufacturer's instructions.
Specialist Asian ingredients are available in large
supermarkets, Thai, Chinese, Japanese and
Vietnamese shops, as well as Asian stores.

Designer
Robin Rout
Editor
Elsa Petersen-Schepelern
Editorial Assistant
Maddalena Bastianelli
Publishing Director
Anne Ryland
Production
Patricia Harrington

Food Stylist
Alastair Hendy
Cooking Assistant
Kate Habershon
Stylist
Alastair Hendy
Author Photograph
David Loftus

contents

Red tomatoes, purple aubergines, yellow corn, blue berries and white peaches are summer's primaries, the season's culinary building blocks. Fast food ingredients full of vibrant flavour, ripe for endless ideas, they are nature's perfect packages, all perfectly nutritious and perfectly delicious. Mixed with other fresh ingredients, their flavours dazzle and shine. A sun-ripened tomato can be enjoyed mashed onto garlic-rubbed toast with a smattering of sea salt, pepper and good splash of olive oil. Or a sunny cob of corn smothered with melting salty butter and masses of freshly crushed black pepper – the more the better. Sugar-dusted berries with a spoon of mascarpone. A perfectly ripe peach, saturated with flavour, just as it is – as nature intended. No knives, no forks, just fingers.

I've kept things simple and to the point. While shopping for ingredients for this book I had to make changes according to what I could find and was at the peak of freshness, so do the same when shopping for my recipes. Change a vegetable or two, according to what you find; if something you see looks really good, buy it, and work it in somewhere.

Nothing is written in stone – your adaptation may work better than mine. It's an instinctual thing. There are lots of serving ideas in this book, but you don't have to present the food the way I have. It all tastes good, and that's what real food is all about. That's the point.

I haven't filled these pages with leafy salads. Though it's summer and the accent on eating is light, we all have our favourite salad ingredients, and the best salads have simple dressings.

So enjoy summer with the recipes and ideas enclosed. Eat outside in the garden or on the verandah. Or pack a picnic and go for the great outdoors. Anywhere, any way, with fresh ingredients like these, your food will taste wonderful.

Finding a tomato that tastes of tomato is difficult these days. Out of season, it's impossible. In season, and grown on home soil, enriched with summer sun, they should taste sweet yet sharp and be densely fleshed with heady scent and a liquid nectar centre. Smell and texture, for me, are all part of a good tomato experience. So stick to summer, check their origin, sniff them out, literally. Don't be seduced by perfection. Blemishes and quirky shapes are the true nature of tomato taste. Plum tomatoes are a good example. When they first appeared in supermarkets they used to look like proper plum tomatoes, like the ones piled high in Mediterranean markets – glowing, gnarled and fattened, full of sun concentrate and charm. Now, they've often been genetically modified or bred into wishy-washy regularity and a pale imitation of their former selves – you'll get more flavour from a can of good plum tomatoes.

But there is light at the end of the poly-tunnel. For salads, forget the big tomatoes and opt for the babies. Baby ones, on or off the vine, and labelled as 'cherry tomatoes' are best. And there are baby plum tomatoes too, deep scarlet globules of true 'plum' deliciousness; perfect when briefly roasted in a hot oven with a drop of olive oil, and tossed with basil leaves, sea salt and black pepper and served as a salad or piled onto toast. No fancy business – let the tomato flavour shine through. Good tomatoes don't need fuss.

And before I forget, don't bung your tomatoes in the fridge with the rest of the salad ingredients. Try to keep them at their natural temperature (over 12°C) – cold ruins their flavour and there's nothing worse than eating a chilled tomato. We've all got our favourite ways with this fruit (strange to think of it that way), but here, in case you're wondering what you might do next, are a few more...

matoes

Tomato and pepper soup

with aubergine croutons

It's important to use good, well-flavoured tomatoes for this soup – use Italian plum or the so called 'vine-ripened' varieties. Water is used instead of stock, to keep the flavours clean and sharp – perfect for the strict non-meat eaters.

4 large red peppers, preferably the long, tapered Italian variety

5 tablespoons olive oil

1 large onion, chopped

2 garlic cloves, halved

1 kg tomatoes, chopped

leaves and stalks from 6 sprigs of coriander (preferably with roots) or basil

a pinch of sugar

1 teaspoon Tabasco (optional)

1 aubergine, quartered lengthways, inner flesh discarded, flesh cut into small cubes

salt and freshly ground black pepper

Serves 4

1

Put the peppers directly on the gas flame. Turn every minute or so until blackened and blistered all over. Alternatively roast in a preheated oven at 220ºC (425ºF) Gas 7 for 20 minutes. Put them in a covered bowl and let cool. Scrape off the charred skin, then core and deseed the flesh.

2

Heat 2 tablespoons olive oil in a frying pan, add the onion and garlic and sauté until softened and transparent. Add the peppers, tomatoes, herb stalks, sugar, salt and pepper. Stew gently for 20 minutes, then add 400 ml water and stew for a further 20 minutes.

3

Sieve the mixture into a clean saucepan, pushing through all the flesh, and discarding the skins and seeds. Add the Tabasco, if using, warm through (but don't boil), then serve.

4

Season the aubergine then heat the remaining oil in the frying pan. Add the aubergine and fry until golden. Add to the bowls of soup and top with coriander or basil leaves.

Variations:

Add chopped black olives and basil or avocado, or sautéed courgette, or even fried squid or feta cheese at the same time as the aubergine. Alternatively, omit the peppers from the recipe and serve the soup chilled with a Bloody Mary salsa (chopped avocado, tomatoes and coriander, with grated red onion, lime juice and vodka).

Roasted tomatoes in herb oil

with char-grilled bread and baby mozzarella

I love it when restaurants give you a saucer of olive oil and balsamic vinegar plus bread and a few olives – just to keep your stomach occupied while you make a decision over the menu. It looks good, needs virtually no preparation, and tastes great – so why not do it at home. Keep it as simple as that, or add sliced tomato and a few basil leaves, or do a little extra preparation, and try this idea – dishes to dip into or pile on to grilled bread – a self-assembly toast. This barely needs a recipe.

8 small to medium tomatoes

2–4 tablespoons chopped herbs, such as basil, dill, parsley, oregano, marjoram and/or chives

2 tablespoons virgin olive oil

1 ciabatta loaf, sliced

1 fat garlic clove, halved

1 teaspoon balsamic vinegar

4 baby buffalo mozzarella or 1 buffalo mozzarella, cut into chunks

sea salt flakes and coarsely crushed black pepper

Serves 4

1

Roast the tomatoes in a preheated oven at 220°C (425°F) Gas 7 for about 8 minutes. Cool, peel and put in a bowl.

2

Mix the herbs with the oil, pour over the tomatoes and let stand for a few hours or overnight.

3

When ready to serve, grill the slices of bread on both sides then rub with the cut garlic clove. Put the sea salt and pepper in separate small dishes.

4

Drain the tomatoes and reserve the oil. Put the tomatoes in 1 small dish and strain the oil into another, adding a splash of balsamic vinegar. Add a small dish of the mozzarella.

5

Make up your own toast at the table, or eat the tomato and mozzarella separately and dip the toast in the balsamic oil.

Variations:

Add extra dishes, such as jars of vegetable antipasto and cured meats from a delicatessen.
Serve other dishes such as salami, prosciutto, semi-dried tomatoes (page 22), roasted vine tomatoes and bean salad (page 14) or char-grilled aubergine (page 51).

Roasted vine tomatoes

with cannellini bean salad and tapenade oil

Tomatoes grow on bushes, not vines, yet we call tomatoes sold on the stem 'vine tomatoes', probably because they look vaguely like a bunch of grapes. Roasted on their stems, they keep that just-picked look on the plate.

4 'vines' of baby tomatoes, about 6 fruit each

virgin olive oil, for brushing and dressing

400 g canned cannellini beans, rinsed and drained

½ red onion, finely chopped

1 garlic clove, crushed

2 tablespoons coarsely chopped flat leaf parsley or torn basil leaves

1 tablespoon ready-made tapenade*

½ teaspoon sugar

juice of ½ lemon

sea salt and cracked black pepper

Serves 4

*Tapanade, or olive paste, is available in Italian delicatessens and larger supermarkets.

1

Arrange the tomato 'vines' in a single layer on a baking sheet, brush with olive oil and sprinkle with salt and pepper. Roast in a preheated oven at 220°C (425°F) Gas 7 for 6–8 minutes, until the skins have lightly blistered.

2

Put the beans, onion, garlic, parsley and tapenade in a bowl and stir gently. Dissolve the sugar in the lemon juice and add to the bean mixture. Stir in about 2 tablespoons olive oil and let stand at room temperature for 30 minutes.

3

To serve, spread the bean salad over serving plates, add a 'vine' of tomatoes to each plate, spoon over any remaining bean dressing and tomato roasting juices and dress liberally with more olive oil.

Variations:

Make into a more substantial course by adding flakes of blackened salmon (page 22), roasted cod, fried mullet or barbecued monkfish kebabs.
Give it the niçoise treatment and mix the tapenade with mayonnaise, add halved boiled eggs, anchovies and rare-roasted tuna.

Tomato and pimiento tart

Pimientos are large, heart-shaped peppers (not to be confused with pimento or Jamaican allspice). If you can't find them, make this tart with tomatoes only (buy 2 punnets extra). Yoghurt cheese needs a bit of planning and this quantity of yoghurt makes more than you'll need for this tart– use it up on toast or with cheese biscuits. If you don't have time to make your own cheese, use Philadelphia cream cheese instead.

500 ml plain Greek yoghurt

1 teaspoon salt

1 large garlic clove, crushed

3 tablespoons finely chopped mixed fresh herbs, such as parsley, basil, chives, dill and tarragon, plus sprigs for serving

½ packet frozen puff pastry (210 g), thawed

1 punnet cherry tomatoes (about 20)

3 canned pimientos, or red peppers drained, deseeded and sliced lengthways

1 egg, lightly beaten, to glaze

Serves 4

Variations:

Spread the pastry with a layer of tapenade and top with tomatoes.
Cover with sliced tomatoes, bake, and serve with fresh pesto.
Flavour the yoghurt cheese with toasted cumin seeds, sprinkle with paprika and eat with toast.

1

Two days in advance, mix the yoghurt, salt and garlic in a small bowl or jug. Place a large square of muslin in a large bowl and pour in the yoghurt mixture. Gather up the corners and sides and tie tightly with string. Tie the bundle to a long-handled spoon and suspend over a deep container. Chill in the refrigerator for 2 days to allow the whey to drain from the yoghurt.

2

When ready to cook, discard the whey, put the yoghurt cheese into a bowl and mix in the chopped herbs.

3

Roll out the pastry to a rectangle or circle and spread with half the cheese, leaving a 1 cm border around the edges. Top with the whole baby tomatoes and strips of pimiento. Brush the edges of the pastry with beaten egg.

4

Bake in a preheated oven at 220°C (425°F) Gas 7 for 35 minutes or until the pastry has risen and is golden. Scatter with herbs and serve hot.

17

Summer lasagne

This isn't a regular baked lasagne: it's much lighter, like a dressed summer pasta – a light and fruity tomato salsa with courgette and basil, under a blanket of ricotta and pasta.

6 sprigs of basil

5 tablespoons fruity virgin olive oil

2 strips of lemon peel

2 strips of orange peel

500 g ripe red tomatoes, skinned, deseeded and chopped*

2 sun-dried tomato halves (in oil), very finely sliced

6 baby globe courgettes, halved, or 2 regular courgettes halved and thickly sliced and blanched in salted boiling water

350 g ricotta, at room temperature

12 sheets lasagne pasta, green or plain

salt and freshly ground black pepper

Serves 4

1

Remove the basil leaves from the stems and reserve. Tear half the leaves and keep the remainder whole. Warm the oil in a small saucepan with the basil stems and citrus peel. Remove and discard the stems and peel.

2

Add the tomatoes, sun-dried tomatoes, salt and pepper, then stir in the courgettes. Heat gently for about 1 minute. Stir in the chopped basil just before serving. Season the ricotta.

3

Cook the lasagne in a wide saucepan of salted boiling water until just soft – move and separate the sheets as they cook. (You will need 12 sheets, but some may tear or stick together.) Carefully drain the lasagne, then hang the sheets around the edges of the colander so they don't stick together.

4

To assemble the lasagne, make free-form layers of all the ingredients on each serving plate, dress with any remaining infused oil and sprinkle with salt and freshly ground pepper.

*Note: Prick the tomatoes all over, put in a bowl and cover with boiling water for 2 minutes. Drain. The skins will slip off easily.

Variations:

Use roasted vine cherry tomatoes instead of chopped tomatoes (page 14).

Green tomato and basil curry

This is a thin, soup-like curry. The sharpness of the tart green tomatoes is perfect with the sweet and salt flavours of the curry. If green tomatoes are unavailable, use under ripe ones instead, adding them to the pan about 5 minutes before the end of cooking.

750 g green tomatoes, quartered

a handful of basil leaves, chopped, plus extra for serving

5 tablespoons virgin olive oil

400 ml canned coconut milk

½ tablespoon fish sauce

2 teaspoons sugar

salt and freshly ground black pepper

Curry paste

4 large mild green chillies, chopped

5 hot green chillies, chopped

5 shallots, chopped

5 garlic cloves

3 cm ginger, chopped

1 stalk lemongrass, trimmed, outer casing discarded, chopped

6 kaffir lime leaves, finely chopped, or 1 teaspoon finely chopped lime zest

2 teaspoons shrimp paste (*blachan*), or anchovy essence

Serves 4

***Note:** Shrimp paste is a salty Indonesian seasoning. If unavailable, omit it or use anchovy essence instead.*

1

Put all the ingredients for the curry paste into a food processor or blender and work to a paste. Add 2 of the quartered tomatoes and purée again.

2

Mix the chopped basil in a bowl with 3 tablespoons of the olive oil.

3

Heat the remaining oil in a wok or wide, shallow saucepan, add the paste and stir-fry until the oil separates – about 4 minutes.

4

Add the coconut milk, fish sauce, sugar, salt, pepper and 300 ml water. Bring to the boil, reduce the heat and simmer for about 15 minutes. Add the tomato quarters and gently simmer for a further 10 minutes. Stir in the basil-flavoured oil and serve with whole basil leaves on top – and plenty of plain boiled rice.

Variations:

Before serving, you could stir in some fresh pesto, made without Parmesan – the creamy pine nuts add an extra dimension to the taste and texture, not dissimilar to the crushed nuts used in many Asian curry pastes.
Other possible additions include thin strips of stir-fried beef or chicken and other vegetables, such as Thai wing beans or dwarf beans. Use coriander instead of basil.
Make a red tomato curry using red tomato and red chillies instead of green, adding whole cherry tomatoes 5 minutes before the end of cooking.

Blackened salmon
with semi-dried tomato salad

I like my salmon undercooked. Opaque, moist and succulent. And this is it – perfect salmon in a matter of minutes. Serve it warm or at room temperature. Semi-dried tomatoes taste like a cross between roasted and sun-dried tomatoes: the slow drying process concentrates the tomato flavour and much improves fresh tomatoes low on flavour.

8 plum tomatoes, quartered

4 teaspoons dried oregano

600 g thick salmon fillet, skin on

1 teaspoon paprika

1 garlic clove, crushed

sea salt and freshly ground black pepper

olive oil, for brushing

Dressing:

4 tablespoons virgin olive oil

1 teaspoon balsamic vinegar

Serves 4

1

Put the quartered tomatoes on a baking sheet lined with baking parchment. Sprinkle with half the oregano, salt and pepper, and brush with olive oil. Put into the oven on the bottom shelf of the oven and set to 100°C (200°F) Gas ½. Leave to dry for about 2–3 hours. Check them occasionally in case they dry too fast.

2

Rub the flesh side of the salmon fillet with the remaining oregano, paprika, garlic, salt and pepper, and then brush all over with olive oil.

3

Heat a heavy, iron frying pan (preferably non-stick) until smoking hot. Add the salmon, flesh side down, and sear without moving it for 2 minutes. Turn it over (it should look blackened) and cook for a further 3 minutes: it should be rare in the middle. Remove the skin and flake the flesh into large chunks.

4

To serve, put the flaked salmon and the oven-dried tomatoes on 4 plates. Mix the dressing ingredients together and sprinkle over each serving.

Variations:

Add torn lettuce leaves, such as batavia (escarole) or cos, chopped avocado and fine beans.
Serve with the tapenade cannellini beans (page 14).
Use semi-dried tomatoes with grilled vegetables and basil to make a ratatouille salad, or use them in aubergine mozzarella lasagne (page 47).

22

Corn, believe it or not, makes our world go round. We consume it without knowing it. Most of the world's crop goes into products that shape our everyday lives from toothpaste to tablets, from detergents and paper to glue. It's used to stabilize and add body to processed and canned foods, and to assist pourability – coating sugars and grains so they flow readily. Next time you dust your biscuits with icing sugar or refill the salt shaker, think about it.

But it's the fresh corn cob, jammed with sweet summer kernels, that inspires the cook and holds the most dynamic flavour. Corn, maize, sweetcorn (call it what you will) is the outsized fruit of an outsized grass with an exceptionally vibrant taste – sweet, smooth and warm all at the same time. It's good on its own, picked straight from the plant and eaten immediately, raw – the sugars have had no time to turn to starch, so it's very tender and sweet. Baby corn or candle corn is another variety, bred in an attempt to bring corn down to an acceptable colour and polite size – a pale imitation of the parent's fuller figure and flavour. Not good.

Sweetcorn is the variety grown to be eaten fresh, but there are others. Dent corn has a starchy kernel and is ground to make cornmeal and polenta (made from soft dent); flint has hard hulls and is used for polenta; popcorn has a very hard husk that pops when heat is applied and the starch within expands dramatically; and a variety that's grown just to make flour, masa, used to make tortillas and tamales. Some of the best recipes for corn come from America, its homeland – thick fish chowders, homely johnnycakes, breakfast grits and bean stews like succotash.

'Corn on the cob' is this vegetable's signature dish – the one we all know and love. You can't beat it, boiled or barbecued, with lots of melted butter and freshly cracked black pepper. I tend to get carried away with the pepper mill and am a bit excessive with the butter. But that's what a corn on the cob is there for, isn't it? Remember – don't salt the cooking water – this will toughen the kernels: just salt them before serving. And if you feel the cobs are too big, cut them into sections. The jolly giant grass with golden fruit makes far more than a bowl of cornflakes. It's big and bright and always steals the show. So let it.

corn

Grilled corn

with chilli butter and black pepper

Chipotles – dried, smoked jalapeño chillies – are the aristocrats of the chilli world, with wonderful, complex flavour from the hickory wood used for smoking. Chillies are one of the glories of Mexican cooking and form the perfect marriage with that other New World ingredient, corn.

4 chipotle chillies or other mild dried chillies
or 2 small fresh red chillies, very finely chopped

125 g butter, at room temperature

½ teaspoon freshly ground cumin

1 teaspoon dried oregano

4 fresh corn cobs

salt and plenty freshly ground black pepper

Serves 4

1

If using dried chillies, soak them in warm water for 20 minutes before using. When soft, split open, discard the seeds and chop the flesh finely.

2

Mash the butter with the chilli, cumin and oregano.

3

Cook the corn in boiling water for about 8 minutes, then drain. Heat a stove-top grill pan or barbecue until very hot, then cook on all sides until flecked with black.

4

Rub with a generous amount of the chilli butter, sprinkle with salt and plenty of pepper, and serve.

Corn and sweet potato bhajia

with hot and sour sambal

Don't be put off by the long list of ingredients – everything is easily put together. The sambal is not compulsory, but it is the business: it contains all the flavours of Indonesian cooking, salt, hot, sour and sweet, all in one dip. If you don't have time, serve the bhajia (plural of bhaji) with soy sauce instead.

2 fresh corn cobs

1 sweet potato, finely sliced or grated

90 g plain flour

4 small shallots, finely sliced

12 spring onions, finely sliced lengthways

3 tablespoons chopped fresh coriander

3 cm fresh ginger, grated

1 garlic clove, crushed

2 small red chillies

1 teaspoon sugar

vegetable oil, for frying

Sambal:

1 stalk lemongrass, trimmed and finely chopped

1 garlic clove, crushed

3 red chillies, finely sliced

1 teaspoon shrimp paste (*blachan*), (optional)

1 tablespoon peanut oil

3 teaspoons caster sugar

4 tomatoes, deseeded and chopped

2 tablespoons *kecap manis* (Indonesian ketchup) or dark soy sauce

1 tablespoon tamarind paste mixed with 3 tablespoons water or 2 tablespoons lime juice with 2 tablespoons water

1 tablespoon crushed toasted peanuts, to serve (optional)

Serves 4

1

To make the sambal, mix together the lemongrass, garlic, chillies and shrimp paste and fry in the peanut oil for about 1 minute. Stir in the remaining ingredients and 100 ml warm water and let cool. Serve in a small dish, sprinkled with crushed toasted peanuts, if using.

2

Meanwhile, to make the bhajia, first cook the corn in a large saucepan of boiling water for 8 minutes. Drain, then hold the corn vertically on a board and slice off the kernels. Discard the core.

3

Mix the corn, sweet potato, flour, shallots, spring onions, coriander, ginger, garlic, chillies and sugar in a bowl to form a thick batter.

4

Heat the oil in a large frying pan, add tablespoons of the mixture and fry in small batches until golden on both sides. Serve the bhajia with the sambal.

Corn congee

with vinegared crab, ginger and crisp glass noodles

Congee is a thick rice soup, popular throughout Asia, and has all sorts of things served with it and in it to pep it up, depending on the time of day it is eaten. It's the muddled balance of all these that makes congee taste good.

500 g short grain rice, soaked for at least 2 hours

2 litres light chicken stock

1 teaspoon salt

a handful of cooked corn kernels

250 g white crab meat

100 g glass noodles (beanthread vermicelli)

peanut or corn oil, for frying

Dressing:

3 tablespoons rice vinegar

2 tablespoons rice wine or mirin

2 teaspoons caster sugar

1 small red chilli, finely sliced

½ teaspoon salt or 1 tablespoon fish sauce

Serves 4

To serve (optional):

your choice of: fish sauce, soy sauce, fresh coriander, 3 cm fresh ginger, finely grated, poached chicken, chopped prawns, dried shrimp or sliced barbecued Chinese pork

1

Put the rice, chicken stock and salt in a saucepan and bring to the boil. Reduce the heat and simmer for 1 hour or until the grains have disintegrated. Top up with boiling water if the soup becomes too thick. Taste and adjust the seasoning. Add the corn and cook for a further 10 minutes.

2

To make the dressing, mix the rice vinegar, rice wine, sugar, chilli and salt or fish sauce in a bowl and stir until the sugar has dissolved, then use one-third of the mixture to dress the crab.

3

Heat 2 tablespoons of oil in a wok or frying pan, add the glass noodles straight from the packet, and fry for a few seconds until they become puffy and crisp.

4

Serve the congee in 4 rice bowls set on 4 large plates. Divide the crab between the plates. Serve with the noodles and separate bowls of your choice of the fish sauce, soy sauce, coriander, ginger, chicken, prawns, dried shrimp, pork and remaining dressing in separate bowls, adding different condiments to your spoon with every mouthful.

Seafood and corn gumbo

Gumbo is the Louisiana classic thickened with filé (ground sassafras leaves) or chopped okra and usually made with seafood, although chicken, duck and boudin sausage can be used too. My version is more like a *marinière* (no self-respecting Louisiana cook would add wine) – but it tastes brilliant anyway.

750 g mixed seafood, such as mussels or clams, prawns or squid, or lobster

1 fresh corn cob

3 tablespoons olive oil

½ teaspoon chilli flakes

3 garlic cloves, crushed

3 shallots, chopped

2 carrots, diced

2 teaspoons coriander seeds

200 ml white wine

400 ml chicken stock

juice of 1 lime

a pinch of saffron

4 tomatoes, quartered

200 g okra

1 tablespoon chopped parsley

1 tablespoon chopped thyme

salt and freshly ground black pepper

To serve:

fresh coriander sprigs

char-grilled bread or boiled rice

Serves 4

1

Scrub the mussels or clams and discard any that remain open.

2

Boil the corn in unsalted water for about 8 minutes and either cut into chunks or slice the kernels off the cob.

3

Put the squid, prawns, if using, and 1 tablespoon of the oil in a bowl with the chilli flakes, salt, pepper and half the garlic. Heat a frying pan until smoking hot and sear the squid and prawns or lobster for 1 minute. Remove from the pan and set aside.

4

Heat the remaining oil in the pan, add the shallots, carrots, coriander seeds and remaining garlic and sauté until softened but not browned. Add the wine, stock, lime juice and saffron and simmer for 5 minutes. Add the mussels or clams, corn, tomatoes and okra and simmer gently for a further 5 minutes. Add the remaining seafood, parsley and thyme, then taste and adjust the seasoning. Cook for a further 2 minutes.

5

Divide the gumbo between 4 heated bowls, top with coriander and serve with grilled bread or boiled rice.

Southern fried chicken

stuffed with ham and cheese, served with corn salad

The good thing about this is that the chicken portions can be fried well before they're needed, then heated in the oven until crisp.

4 free-range chicken legs, skinned and boned*

180 g grated mozzarella or mild cheddar cheese

4 thin slices cooked ham

plain flour, for dusting

1 egg, lightly beaten

6 tablespoons dried or fresh breadcrumbs

30 g butter

olive oil, for brushing and frying

salt and freshly ground black pepper

Honey and lime corn salad:

2 fresh corn cobs

½ teaspoon honey

juice of 1 lime

10 cherry tomatoes

6 spring onions, halved and finely sliced lengthways

leaves from small bunch of fresh coriander, chopped

2 tablespoons soured cream

jalapeño (green) Tabasco, to taste

salt and freshly ground black pepper

Serves 4

*****Note:** To bone the legs, start from the 'hip', separating the meat from the bone with the tip of a sharp knife. Follow the bone, keeping the flesh intact until you reach the 'knee'. Roll back the flesh and carefully scrape the meat from around the cartilage – don't worry about making a few holes. Proceed half way down the next bone, fold back the meat and cut off the bone. A small 'handle' of bone will remain. (Your butcher may do this job for you.)*

1

To prepare the corn salad, cook the corn cobs for 8 minutes in boiling water. Rub the cobs with olive oil and seasoning and sear in a preheated hot frying pan until tinged with a few black speckles. Using a sharp knife, slice the kernels off the cob and reserve.

2

Rub the boned chicken legs inside and out with salt and pepper. Roll the cheese up in the ham and stuff each leg with a ham-cheese roll. Fold over the thigh flap of flesh to enclose the stuffing and secure with a cocktail stick. Dust each leg with flour, dip into the beaten egg, then roll in the breadcrumbs. Pat on extra crumbs over any bald patches.

3

Heat 5 mm of olive oil and the butter in an ovenproof frying pan and fry the chicken legs on both sides, about 5 minutes on each side, until golden brown. Transfer to a preheated oven and roast at 190ºC (375ºF) Gas 5 for 15–20 minutes.

4

Dissolve the honey in a bowl with the lime juice, then stir in the corn, tomatoes, spring onions, coriander, soured cream, Tabasco, salt and pepper. Divide the mixture between 4 plates or bowls, top with the chicken and serve.

Polenta crust chicken

with avocado corn cream and balsamic-chilli dip

Polenta is the Italian version of cornmeal, and also the dish made from it, either a creamy purée or a grilled cake. The raw ingredient makes a delicious alternative to a breadcrumb coating, giving a toasted corn flavour to the main dish. Use golden corn-fed chicken to complete the picture.

4 corn-fed chicken breasts, skin on

6 tablespoons instant polenta flour or cornmeal

plain flour, for dusting

1 egg, lightly beaten

vegetable oil, for frying

2 spring onions, halved and finely sliced lengthways, to serve

Avocado corn cream:

300 g cooked corn kernels

4 spring onions, chopped

1 garlic clove, crushed

1 small ripe avocado

juice of ½ lemon

1 tablespoon olive oil

salt and freshly ground pepper

Balsamic-chilli dip:

2 tablespoons sweet chilli sauce

2 tablespoons balsamic vinegar

Serves 4

1

Season the chicken breasts and polenta flour or cornmeal with salt and freshly ground black pepper. Dust the breasts with plain flour, dip in the egg and then roll in the polenta flour (pat on extra if there are any gaps). Chill for about 30 minutes.

2

To make the corn cream, put the corn in a food processor and blend to a purée. Add the spring onions, garlic, avocado flesh, lemon juice, oil, salt and pepper and work again to a purée.

3

Mix the chilli sauce and balsamic vinegar and put in a small dipping bowl.

4

Heat about 1 cm depth of oil in a large frying pan, add the chicken, cover with a lid and gently fry for about 6–8 minutes on each side.

5

Slice the chicken into wedges and serve with the avocado corn cream, the balsamic-chilli dip and finely sliced spring onion.

Variations:

Roll up with salad leaves in flour or corn tortillas. Layer into toasted club sandwiches.

Aubergines look voluptuous, their nightshade colours and silky sheen lend an air of forbidden fruit. And once they were. They belong to the same family as tomatoes and deadly nightshade, *Solanaceae*, and were once thought poisonous. The people of India knew better. They were doing delicious things with them well before the West. We caught on a few hundred years later. These days, there are many varieties; the familiar large purple, the long thin Mediterranean or Asian kinds, the round ones streaked with violet or white, the smooth-skinned white, egg-shaped version responsible for the American name of eggplant. In Thailand, there are even more; small yellow, white or green and white, with crunch and a slight bitter taste, and sharp-tasting pea aubergines that grow in bunches like grapes.

White fleshed and silky smooth when cooked, aubergines absorb oil massively. Like sponges, they will soak up as much as you might care to give them.

There are various approaches to avoid an oil overdose: try cutting them into slices then brushing with oil on both sides before char-grilling or roasting. You can also fry them in oil, then leave to drain in a colander, or dip the slices in flour and egg before frying so the batter acts as an oil barrier. Aubergines have little flavour of their own, and this is what makes them so versatile – they readily adopt whatever flavourings you like to add. Try Indian spices, Mediterranean dressings or Middle Eastern herb mixes.

And finally, to salt or not to salt? Cookery books used to advise slicing and salting before cooking to draw out bitter juices. I can only speculate that the bitterness must have been bred out of them – I haven't encountered a bitter aubergine yet, except the Thai ones, and they're supposed to be a touch sharp.

aub

ergines

Aubergine tempura
with white radish salad and amber dipping sauce

It's a fact – aubergines soak up oil – but dipping slices in batter before frying will prevent this habit. The aubergine comes out perfectly cooked – soft and melting with a crunchy exterior.

2 aubergines

1 daikon (mooli or white radish), grated, preferably on a mandoline

½ tablespoon black sesame seeds (toasted in a dry frying pan)

vegetable oil, for frying

Tempura batter:

2 egg yolks

500 ml iced water

250 g plain flour, reserve 2 tablespoons for dusting

1 teaspoon salt

2 teaspoons bonito flakes (optional)*

Amber sauce:

3 cm fresh ginger, grated then squeezed to extract the juice

3 tablespoons dark soy sauce

3 tablespoons mirin (sweet rice wine)

Serves 4

*****Note:** Bonito flakes are sold in Japanese and other Asian shops.*

1

Quarter the aubergines lengthways and cut each quarter in half crossways. Slice off the core from each piece, leaving a wedge of aubergine about 10–15 mm thick. Slice 'fingers' into each wedge, forming fan shapes.

2

To make the amber dipping sauce, mix the ginger juice, soy sauce and mirin in a small bowl. Put the daikon in a second bowl and sprinkle with the sesame seeds.

3

Make the batter just before it's needed. Beat the egg yolks with the iced water. Tip the flour, salt and bonito flakes, if using, into the water mixture and stir briefly – the batter should be lumpy and not properly mixed.

4

Heat the vegetable oil to about 190°C (375°F). Dust the aubergine fans with flour, dip into the tempura batter, then straight into the hot oil. Deep-fry until crisp then drain on kitchen paper. Serve with the white radish salad and the amber dipping sauce.

Variations:

Deep-fry other vegetables and herbs dipped in batter, for example mint sprigs, courgette flowers, sweet potato, okra and shiitake mushrooms and seafood such as sliced fish fillets, whitebait, prawns or squid.

Pea aubergine laksa with prawns

Pea aubergines, sold in Thai shops, are pea-sized and grow in bunches. They have a tart taste and light crunch. A laksa is a Malay curry with noodles. It can be kept simple with just rice vermicelli noodles and fresh herbs or made more elaborate, by adding seafood, fish cakes and condiments.

125 ml peanut or corn oil

1 stalk lemongrass, trimmed and smashed

600 ml canned coconut milk

a handful of pea aubergines

150 g rice vermicelli noodles

juice of ½ lime

8 large cooked prawns (optional)

sea salt and freshly ground black pepper

fresh coriander, to serve

Rempah:

50 g macadamia or cashew nuts

8 small shallots, chopped

4 garlic cloves, crushed

2 small red chillies, chopped

2 cm fresh turmeric root, peeled and chopped (optional)*

3 cm fresh galangal or ginger, chopped

2 teaspoons chopped coriander root or 1 teaspoon coriander seeds

1 teaspoon shrimp paste (*blachan*) or anchovy essence

Serves 4

1

Put all the rempah ingredients in a blender or food processor and blend to a paste. Heat the oil in a saucepan or wok, add the paste and stir-fry until darkened. Strain off the excess oil.

2

Add the lemongrass, 200 ml water and the coconut milk and bring to a fast simmer. When the liquid has reduced and thickened a little, add the pea aubergines and simmer gently for a further 10 minutes.

3

Soak the rice noodles in a bowl of hot water until soft – about 15 minutes. Drain and divide between 4 bowls.

4

Season the soup with lime juice, salt and pepper, then ladle over the noodles. Add plenty of fresh coriander and 2 prawns, if using, to each bowl.

Note: *Turmeric root is available from Asian markets. It doesn't have a great deal of flavour and is mainly used for its colour. The dazzling ochre-coloured juices stain everything, including fingers – so handle with care.*

Variations:

Other cooked seafood, such as squid, octopus, fish pieces, crispy fish cakes, mussels or clams can be added. Other choices are cooked sliced meat or poultry, spicy meat balls, poached egg, other vegetables, crisp shallots and Asian herbs.

43

Indian pickled aubergine

with egg, basil and cardamom rice

This pickle has a gently sweet-sour flavour, not sharp. Eat it hot or cold –(it tastes wonderful either way) or serve with freshly baked focaccia instead of rice, and you have great picnic food. Cook ahead, if you can, and leave for a few hours for the flavours to develop and meld – then reheat before serving.

3 cm fresh ginger, chopped

6 garlic cloves

1 onion, chopped

2 medium aubergines, quartered lengthways, with the central 'seed' core removed

125 ml mustard oil, peanut or corn oil, for frying, plus 1 tablespoon for sautéing

2 teaspoons ground cumin

2 teaspoons lightly crushed coriander seeds

3 teaspoons panchphoran spice mix*

a pinch of cayenne pepper

4 tomatoes, chopped

3 tablespoons red wine vinegar

4 teaspoons jaggery or muscovado sugar

a handful of fresh basil leaves

8 cardamom pods

500 ml basmati rice

salt and freshly ground black pepper

4 hard-boiled eggs, peeled and halved, to serve

Serves 4

1

Put the ginger, garlic and onion in a food processor and work to a coarse paste.

2

Sprinkle the aubergine with salt and pepper. Heat 125 ml of the oil in a frying pan, add half the cumin and coriander seeds and the aubergine. Fry on all sides until lightly golden. Put the aubergine in a colander over a bowl.

3

Tip any collected oil from the aubergine back into the frying pan, heat and add the panchphoran. Fry for a few seconds until the seeds pop. Add the ginger paste, cayenne and the remaining cumin and coriander seeds and fry until the oil separates from the mixture, (adding extra oil if necessary). Add the tomatoes, vinegar and sugar and cook gently for about 10 minutes, stirring occasionally to prevent sticking.

4

Add the fried aubergine to the mixture and cook for a further 5–10 minutes. Add salt and pepper to taste. Keep hot and stir in half the basil just before serving.

5

Heat 1 tablespoon of oil in a deep saucepan, add the cardamom pods and sauté until aromatic. Add the rice and stir to coat the grains with oil. Add salt and 750 ml water, cover and bring to the boil. Reduce the heat and simmer very gently for 8 minutes. Turn off the heat and leave covered for 10 minutes.

6

Spoon the rice into 4 heated bowls, then top with the aubergines, the remaining basil and the halved, hard-boiled eggs.

Variations:

Use fresh coriander or mint instead of basil. Add fresh curry leaves to flavour the curry or along with the cardamom to flavour the rice. Serve the pickled aubergine with pappadams instead of rice or stir a spoonful of melted creamed coconut into the rice just before serving.

Note: *Panchphoran is available from Indian shops. If you can't find it, make your own: mix 2 teaspoons each of black mustard seeds, cumin seeds, nigella (onion) seeds, fennel seeds and fenugreek seeds – it's not imperative that you include all of these, but 'panch' means 'five'.*

Aubergine mozzarella lasagne

This is a no-bake lasagne. All you have to do is pre-cook the pasta and vegetables (a few hours in advance, if you like), then quickly assemble all the components, reheat and serve – a sort of lasagne-in-a-hurry. Fresh and healthy, it looks as if you've spent hours on it.

3 garlic cloves, crushed

1 small bunch of basil, stems and leaves separated

100 ml olive oil

18 sheets lasagne pasta, fresh or dried

2 aubergines, sliced lengthways into 12 slices

1 tablespoon tapenade or sun-dried tomato paste

3 courgettes (yellow and/or green), thinly sliced lengthways, then blanched in salted boiling water

1 mozzarella (preferably buffalo), thinly sliced

salt and freshly ground black pepper

Serves 4

1

Put the garlic, basil stems and olive oil in a saucepan and warm through for about 10 minutes to infuse the flavours.

2

Cook the lasagne in a wide saucepan of salted boiling water until just soft – move and separate the sheets as they cook. (You will need 12 sheets, but some may tear or stick together.) Carefully drain the lasagne, then put it into cold water to stop it overcooking or sticking together. Hang the sheets around the edges of the colander so they don't stick together.

3

Brush the aubergine slices on both sides with some of the infused oil. Cook in a preheated stove-top grill pan or frying pan until seared and soft.

4

To assemble, arrange 4 slices of aubergine across a baking sheet. Top each slice with a sheet of lasagne, spread a little tapenade or tomato paste on each, then add a slice of courgette and mozzarella, and a couple of basil leaves. Repeat with all the ingredients, until you have 4 multi-storey piles of pasta, vegetables and mozzarella. Brush all over with more of the infused oil, cover loosely with foil and heat through in a preheated oven at 220°C (425°F) Gas 7 for about 5 minutes or until the cheese begins to melt.

Variations:

Use semi-dried tomatoes (page 22) instead of sun-dried tomato paste. Alternative layering ingredients include goat's cheese, Parma ham, soft cheese, toasted pine nuts, cumin seeds, roasted red peppers, mint, peas, seared scallops or lemon oil.

Chilli lime fried squid

Thai and violet aubergines with crushed toasted peanuts

Don't give up on the recipe if you can't get the listed aubergines, it will taste very good using ordinary ones. Likewise, use regular limes if kaffirs aren't available. Remember, there are no rules, these recipes are very flexible.

500 g prepared squid
(the fishmonger can do this
for you)

grated zest and juice
of 2 kaffir limes or
1 regular lime

1 tablespoon sugar

1 tablespoon fish sauce

3 garlic cloves, crushed

1 teaspoon chilli flakes

cornflour, for dusting

12 small Thai aubergines,
trimmed and quartered

1 round violet aubergine or
small regular aubergine,
cut into bite-sized pieces

3 cm fresh ginger, sliced

peanut or corn oil, for
frying

1 teaspoon *kecap manis*
(Indonesian ketchup) or
2 teaspoons dark soy sauce

To serve:

a few salad leaves

2 tablespoons crushed
peanuts, toasted in a dry
frying pan

Serves 4

1

Slice the squid into fine rings and separate the ring of tentacles. Put in a bowl and mix in the lime zest and juice, the sugar, fish sauce, garlic and chilli flakes. Let stand for at least 30 minutes.

2

Remove the squid from the marinade and dust with cornflour. Add the aubergines and ginger to the marinade and toss well.

3

Heat a shallow pool of oil in a wok or deep frying pan. Fry the squid in batches for about 1 minute until lightly golden and crisp. Drain on kitchen paper and keep hot while you cook the remainder.

4

Tip away most of the oil in the wok, leaving about 3–4 tablespoons. Add the aubergine and *kecap manis* or dark soy sauce and stir-fry for 1 minute.

5

To serve, divide the aubergine between 4 plates or bowls, top with the squid, a few salad leaves and the crushed toasted peanuts.

Lamb burgers

with char-grilled aubergine, hoummus, seed salt and mint

Homemade burgers are vastly superior to shop-bought ones, and so easy to make that we should all make them more often – everyone loves a burger. The seed salt is delicious – store the extra and use it in lots of other ways.

2 tablespoons olive oil, plus extra for brushing

1 onion, finely chopped

2 cloves garlic, crushed

1 small chilli, very finely chopped (optional)

500 g lamb mince

a handful of mint leaves, chopped, plus extra leaves to serve

1 aubergine, sliced lengthways

sea salt and freshly ground black pepper

150 g hoummus, to serve

Seed salt:

1 tablespoon cumin seeds

1 tablespoon sesame seeds

1 tablespoon sea salt

Makes 6 burgers

1

To make the seed salt, toast the cumin seeds and sesame seeds in a dry frying pan until the sesame seeds are a light golden brown (watch them, and turn them regularly – they'll burn if left alone). Mix in a bowl with the salt.

2

Heat half the olive oil in the frying pan, add the onion, garlic, chilli, 2 teaspoons seed salt and black pepper and sauté until the onion is soft and transparent.

3

Put the lamb mince in a bowl with the chopped mint, the onion mixture, salt and freshly ground black pepper. Mix well. Shape into burgers, brush with oil and cook under a hot grill or in a preheated stove-top grill pan until crisp and brown outside and pink in the middle. Remove and drain on kitchen paper.

4

Brush the aubergine slices on both sides with the remaining oil and season with salt and pepper. Char-grill on both sides until seared with black lines and softened.

5

Serve the lamb burgers topped with a spoonful of hoummus and a fold of aubergine, sprinkled with a little seed salt and a few mint leaves.

Variations:

To make *baba ganoush*, mash the aubergine with lemon juice, tahini, olive oil, crushed garlic, seed salt and chopped mint – serve with minted lamb meat balls (use burger mixture).

51

In the fruit hierarchy, peaches sit at the top of the ladder, deemed the epitome of perfection in the fruit stakes; the 'perfect peach', unblemished, velvet-smooth and blushing. It's a shy fruit, serene and understated, with sweet flesh that bruises readily. Bruising attacks the fragile cells within and spreads rapidly – the nectar-like juices turn sour and the flesh turns to mush. Perfection is all, so handle with care!

Ripeness, also, is important – peaches should feel firm with a little give and be faintly scented. Anything vaguely green should be avoided as it will remain rock hard – room temperature will only ripen firm fruit of already peach colour. Fruit will be best in peach-growing country, and the longer it stays on the tree before being picked, the better it will taste. From the moment it's picked, it won't get any sweeter. To skin or not to skin? I don't – I'm not into fruit dissection, and it's a fiddly fruit to peel. The warmth of the downy skin against the soft flesh is, to me, all part of the peach-eating experience, and most of the vitamins are stored there. It seems a shame to waste all that goodness and get sticky fingers too. One of the reasons I like peaches so much is that I don't have to peel them. Incidentally, if you want to cut a peach in half to extract the stone neatly, slice around and twist sharply.

The original fruit, a native of China, is still cultivated. It has an outsize stone and very little flesh, but what there is has an unsurpassed taste, and is said to be even better than a white peach. The white peach, I think, is the best variety available, with juicier, more sumptuous flesh than its yellow cousin. But of whatever colour, peaches are one of the reasons I most look forward to summer.

aches

Bali duck

and sour peach salad with lime, chilli and nut vinaigrette

This recipe may look like a lot of work, but it's actually a very easy, stress-free process, and Steps 1 and 2 can be done the day before you want to use it. Cooking the duck this way renders the meat succulent and the skin extra crisp, and most of the fat melts away, so it's very healthy too.

1 small duck, about 1.5 kg

4 cinnamon sticks, broken

15 cloves, coarsely crushed

4 tablespoons uncooked rice

4 cm fresh ginger, sliced

5 tablespoons dark palm sugar or muscovado sugar

kecap manis (Indonesian ketchup) or dark soy sauce

Sour peach salad:

2 tablespoons peanut oil

4 tablespoons lime or kaffir lime juice

1 large garlic clove, crushed

1 small red chilli, very finely sliced

5 small (preferably Thai) shallots, sliced lengthways

2–3 unripe peaches, finely sliced

2 handfuls of beansprouts, rinsed and trimmed

a selection of fresh herbs, such as basil, coriander or mint

1 tablespoon crushed macadamia nuts or peanuts, lightly toasted

a small bunch of garlic chives or spring onions, finely sliced

salt and freshly ground black pepper

Serves 4

1

Remove and discard the excess fat from the duck. Pour boiling water over the skin and pat dry with kitchen paper. Rub the bird with salt and pepper inside and out. Put on a rack in a roasting tin and roast in a preheated oven at 190°C (375°F) Gas 5 for 1 hour. Remove from the oven, cover loosely with foil and let cool.

2

Cut the duck into 4 pieces. Line the base of a steamer with a double thickness of foil. Grind 1 cinnamon stick and 3 cloves together and set aside. Mix the remaining cinnamon and cloves with the rice, ginger and 4 tablespoons sugar. Spread the mixture over the foil. Assemble the steamer and put the roasted duck pieces in the steaming tray, cover and place over a high heat. When you can smell the aroma of spice, turn the heat to low and let smoke gently for about 20 minutes. Discard the rice mixture.

3

Rub the duck with ½ tablespoon sugar and brush with *kecap manis* or soy sauce and the reserved spices. Put on a baking sheet and roast in a preheated oven at 220°C (425°F) Gas 7 for 20 minutes or until crisp and mahogany brown. Shred the meat from the bone.

4

To make the salad, mix the oil, lime juice, garlic, chilli and the remaining sugar in a large bowl until the sugar has dissolved. Stir in the shallots and 1 teaspoon *kecap manis* or soy sauce. Add the sliced peaches, beansprouts, herbs and warm shredded duck and toss well. To serve, pile into bowls and top with toasted crushed nuts and garlic chives.

Squab and peach tagine

Squab are farm-reared pigeons. Their meat is succulent and tender, far superior to wood pigeon. Consequently they're a little expensive and can be difficult to find. Duck breast, guinea fowl pieces or quail will work just as well, but remember to roast the larger birds for longer, about 20 minutes per 500 g, while the quail will only need about 8 minutes.

2 squab (French pigeon)

1 teaspoon ground ginger

½ teaspoon ground cinnamon

1 teaspoon ground mace (optional)

olive oil, for brushing and frying

3 large onions, finely sliced

3 bay leaves

a pinch of saffron (optional)

300 g couscous

chicken stock (see method)

3 garlic cloves, crushed

1 teaspoon paprika

1 teaspoon cumin

1 teaspoon coriander seeds

6 cardamom pods

1 tablespoon pine nuts

2 tablespoons dried muscatels or large raisins

3 firm peaches, sliced into wedges

sea salt and freshly ground black pepper

Serves 4

1

Rub the squab with salt, pepper, ginger, cinnamon and mace, if using. Brush with olive oil and put on a baking sheet. Roast in a preheated oven at 200°C (400°F) Gas 6 for 15 minutes. Remove from the oven and let cool.

2

Slice the breast meat and legs from each bird and set aside. Chop up the wings and carcass and put in a saucepan with 800 ml water. Add half a sliced onion, the bay leaves, salt and pepper. Bring to the boil, then simmer until reduced to about half volume. Strain and discard all the bones. Add the saffron to the strained stock and infuse for about 10 minutes.

3

Put the couscous in a bowl and pour in the stock until the grains are just covered. Let stand for 5 minutes, then fluff up with a fork. Keep it warm.

4

Heat 3 tablespoons olive oil in a frying pan, add the remaining onion and the garlic and sauté until soft and lightly caramelized. Add all the spices, pine nuts and muscatels or raisins and fry for a few minutes more.

5

Spoon the mixture into a shallow saucepan or frying pan with a lid. Pour over the remaining stock. Put a layer of sliced peaches on the top, followed by a layer of squab pieces. Put the lid on the pan and simmer over a low heat for about 10 minutes.

6

Serve on heated dinner plates with separate bowls of saffron couscous.

Vanilla creamed peaches

with frangipane pastries

For pure peach flavour, purée very ripe peaches with the vanilla seeds and leave out the wine – taste and add enough sugar to suit your mood. You could also poach the peaches, then skin them and serve with their juices and the cream. *Frangipane* is a creamed almond paste.

6 peaches

1 bottle white wine (750 ml)

125 g sugar

1 vanilla pod, split lengthways

150 ml double cream, whipped

Frangipane pastries:

250 g puff pastry

200 g white marzipan

icing sugar, for rolling

Serves 4

1

Put the peaches in a saucepan with the white wine, sugar and vanilla pod and bring to the boil. Reduce the heat and simmer for about 20 minutes or until the peaches are soft. Remove them from the syrup and let cool.

2

Discard the skins and stones. Put the flesh in a food processor with a drop of the poaching syrup and blend to make a smooth purée. Chill.

3

To make the frangipane pastries, roll out the pastry to about 5 mm thick. Dust the work surface with icing sugar and roll out the marzipan as thinly as possible. Lay the pastry over the marzipan, then roll up together to make a long sausage shape. Cut the sausage crossways into 1 cm thick slices, then roll or press each one into a flattened oval. Arrange on a baking sheet and cook in a preheated oven at 180°C (350°F) Gas 4 for about 15 minutes or until puffed and tinged golden brown.

4

Spoon the creamed peaches into small bowls, streak cream over the top, and serve with the frangipane pastries for dipping.

Variations:

Spoon the creamed peaches over ice-cream.
Purée with a little Greek honey and serve with Greek yoghurt.
Churn in an ice-cream machine to make sorbet, or mix with the yoghurt and freeze to make ice-cream.

58

Peach and fig almond tart

If peaches are the essence of summer, then figs are its very soul. I love the big purple ones and the little green honey-flavoured variety. I don't skin them, though many people prefer to – I like their colour, especially the purple.

8 sheets filo pastry, or enough to make 4 layers

melted butter, for greasing and brushing

1 tablespoon caster sugar

1 egg, lightly beaten

250 g mascarpone

4 tablespoons ground almonds

4 ripe peaches, pitted and sliced

4 figs, halved or quartered

1 tablespoon dark muscovado sugar, preferably unrefined

Serves 4

Variations:

Substitute other fruits, such as blueberries and plums, nectarines or poached pears.

1

Grease a 35 x 10 cm tranche tin or 22 cm circular tin and line with a single layer of filo pastry (about 2 overlapping sheets). Trim the pastry leaving about 1 cm sticking up above the rim of the tin. Brush with melted butter and line with another 2 sheets of pastry. Repeat until all the pastry has been used.

2

Beat the sugar and egg in a bowl, then beat in the mascarpone and almonds. Spread over the base of the tart.

3

Arrange the pieces of peaches and figs all over the mascarpone cream until the tart case is full. Sprinkle with the muscovado sugar and brush more butter over the pastry and fruit.

4

Put on a baking sheet and bake on the middle shelf of a preheated oven at 200°C (400°F) Gas 6 for 35 minutes or until tinged golden brown.

White peaches in strawberry champagne

The white peach is the queen of peaches and, being a little more expensive than your regular peach, deserves regal treatment. The recipe requires a large number of strawberries, so buy them cheaply at your local market when there's a glut of them at the height of the season. Make sure you cut out any soft bits from the fruit – bad fruit will tarnish the taste.

1

Put the strawberries, sugar and lemon juice into a large saucepan. Place over the lowest heat possible and gently stew for 1 hour. The process is complete when the fruit has turned to an unattractive grey mush and has exuded all its juice.

2

Line a conical sieve with muslin and place over a saucepan. Tip the contents of the pan into the sieve and leave for 2 hours to let the clear red juices run through. Do not be tempted to squeeze the fruit to extract the last few drops. Alternatively, tie up the muslin into a bag, put a wooden spoon through the knot and suspend it over the pan.

3

Discard the muslin and its contents. Add the champagne to the strawberry juice and warm through over a gentle heat. Add the peaches, let cool, then chill. Serve chilled with double cream or crème fraîche.

1.5 kg strawberries

3 tablespoons caster sugar

juice of 1 small lemon

800 ml champagne or other sparkling wine

500 g ripe white peaches, pitted, skinned and finely sliced

double cream, whipped, or crème fraîche, to serve

Serves 4

Variations:

Instead of the peaches, use sliced nectarines and whole strawberries. Serve with chilli and kaffir lime ice (page 65).
To make strawberry champagne jellies, add gelatin (follow packet instructions) to the hot strawberry wine juice, pour into serving bowls, top with peaches and chill.

Blistered peaches with chilli kaffir lime ice

Chilli and kaffir lime ice is addictive. It may sound strange but it works. The sharp iciness of the lime kicks in first and the chilli infusion adds a warming aftertaste. Particularly good with these muscovado caramelized peaches.

4 peaches, halved and pitted

2 tablespoons dark muscovado sugar

1 teaspoon ground allspice

30 g butter, softened

Kaffir lime ice:

5 limes, preferably kaffir limes
(grated zest of 2, juice of 5)

3 small hot chillies, split and deseeded

190 g icing sugar, sieved

450 ml crème fraîche

3 tablespoons iced water

Serves 4

1

To make the ice, put the lime zest and juice, the chillies and icing sugar in a bowl and mix to dissolve the sugar. Set aside for 30 minutes to develop the flavours.

2

Remove and discard the chillies. Beat the crème fraîche thoroughly into the lime syrup. Spoon into a covered container and freeze – there is no need to stir. Remove from the freezer and leave at room temperature for 10 minutes before serving.

3

Just before serving, sprinkle the peach halves with sugar and allspice, then smear over the butter. Lightly brown under a hot grill. Put half a peach in each serving bowl and serve with spoonfuls of ice.

Variations:

For a lighter ice, use whipped double cream instead of crème fraîche.
Serve the ice with fried or grilled bananas, or stir through raspberry purée to make a ripple.
Serve the peaches with crème fraîche beaten with ginger syrup or toasted pine nuts and yoghurt.

65

Summertime is berry time. Sweet downy raspberries, over-stuffed strawberries, velvet-bloomed blueberries, tart gooseberries and sweet beads of white or redcurrants, all eaten straight from the punnet. Our favourites are strawberries, sugar-dusted and swimming in cream. But do you hull them first or not? I must admit I don't, but if you do, make sure you do it after they've been washed – otherwise you'll have waterlogged fruit. Soft berries with a bloom, such as raspberries or blueberries, shouldn't be washed as (like mushrooms) this interferes with their fragile epidermal layers and, apart from losing their velvety texture, they can turn to mush.

When buying berries in the supermarket always check under the container and avoid any with excessive juice – easily identifiable through a plastic punnet. This indicates overripe or bruised fruit. 'Pick your own' berries, where you gather fruit straight from the farmer's field, is the surest route to getting the freshest sun-ripened berries, and with no transportation and refrigeration involved, they taste fantastic. (And you can eat for free as you pick.)

Speaking of food for free, at the end of summer you can pick blackberries and elderberries in the hedgerows. They may need sugar as they can be tart, but are particularly good used in pies, jams or sauces.

Cultivated 'wild' foods, from wild rocket to wild mushrooms, are all the rage. And most fashionable of the berry set are wild strawberries (*fraises des bois*), the American ancestor of the regular strawberry. Dainty, fragrant and oh-so-fragile, they are the caviar of strawberries. Finding them growing wild is now rare but you can buy them from specialist greengrocers. Expensive? Yes. Their shelf life is nil and they go mushy very quickly – so eat them the same day.

Hybrids, such as loganberries, youngberries, boysenberries and tayberries, are the result of crossbreeding raspberries, blackberries or dewberries. In addition, we have golden raspberries and, if you're lucky, white to pale gold cloudberries, found throughout Scandinavia and around the Arctic Circle. Gosh, it's confusing – I'll think I'll stick to the original, the raspberry, a perfectly happy little chap.

berries

Raspberry ripple

Shop-bought ripple is not what it used to be. This one is the real thing and looks the part, with pure vanilla ice-cream, streaked with painterly lines of fresh raspberry purée. A classic combination.

600 ml milk

1 vanilla pod, split lengthways

250 g caster sugar

7 egg yolks

600 ml double cream, whipped to soft peak stage

Ripple:

220 g raspberries, plus extra to serve

60 g caster sugar

1 tablespoon lemon juice

Serves 4

1
Put the milk and vanilla pod in a saucepan. Bring to the boil, remove from the heat and let cool for 30 minutes. Discard the vanilla pod.

2
Beat the sugar and egg yolks in a bowl, then pour in the vanilla milk. Put into a saucepan and heat gently, stirring continuously, until you have a thin custard (too much heat and the custard will curdle and separate). Cool, then chill. Fold the whipped cream into the cold custard, pour into a covered container, then freeze.

3
Put the raspberries, sugar, lemon juice and 1 tablespoon water into a saucepan, bring to the boil, reduce the heat and simmer until soft. Push the mixture through a non-metal sieve into a bowl. Chill.

4
Remove the ice-cream from the freezer and let soften until spreadable. Spoon one-third of the mixture into a shallow square or rectangular container lined with clingfilm. Mark parallel uneven furrows in the ice-cream, then pipe the raspberry purée into the furrows. Carefully spread over another layer of softened ice-cream, repeating until all the ice-cream and raspberry mixture has been used. Finish with more wobbly stripes of ripple. Freeze until set.

5
To serve, remove from the container, discard the clingfilm and trim the sides straight if necessary. Serve alone or with fresh raspberries.

Summer fruit curd

with shortbread biscuits and fresh berries

Sharp and sweet berries, a passionfruit and lemon creamed curd and crumbly shortbread biscuits – the perfect finale for lunch at the end a long summer afternoon. If you really want to be lazy, use a jar of quality lemon curd instead – just stir in some passionfruit juice.

Summer fruit curd:

125 g unsalted butter

220 g caster sugar

sieved flesh from 4 passionfruit

3 lemons

3 eggs, beaten

250 g mascarpone

Shortbread biscuits:

60 g caster sugar

125 g unsalted butter, softened

1 egg yolk

2 teaspoons grated lemon zest

185 g plain flour, sifted

To serve:

4 punnets berries, such as wild strawberries, white, black or red currants, elderberries, raspberries, blackberries or blueberries, about 500 g in total

Makes 8

1

To make the curd, put the butter, sugar and passionfruit pulp into a heatproof bowl with the juice of 1½ lemons and the grated zest of all 3. Fit the bowl over a saucepan of simmering water (the water should not be in contact with the bowl) and stir the mixture until the butter has melted and the sugar dissolved.

2

Add the beaten eggs and stir until the mixture thickens enough to form a film on the back of a spoon. Don't overheat or the mixture may curdle. Let cool.

3

To make the shortbread, mix the sugar, butter, egg yolk and lemon zest in a bowl, then work in the flour to form a smooth dough. If it is too sticky, dust with flour, then work in. Chill for 20 minutes, then roll out the dough and cut out discs with a 5 cm biscuit cutter. Arrange apart on a baking sheet, then bake in a preheated oven at 170°C (325°F) Gas 3 for 30 minutes. Remove from the oven, let cool on the baking sheet for a couple of minutes, then transfer to a wire rack and let cool completely.

4

Beat the curd and mascarpone together until smooth. Serve the curd and berries in separate bowls, accompanied by the biscuits. Alternatively, for an ultra-smart serving idea, cut tracing paper into strips, and curve each strip around a biscuit and secure with tape or a staple. Fill with cream curd, and top with berries.

Golden raspberries with clove chocolate

Golden raspberries taste the same as pink raspberries, but I love their colour – the honey glow of late summer. The clove truffled chocolate can be served as a slab or cut into small cubes – serve them *en masse* on a length of paper with a pile of wooden disposable forks or bamboo skewers. Alternatively, line up the chocolates in a paper-lined box, add some berries and give them as a present.

1

Line a 4 cm deep X 18 cm square cake tin, with clingfilm.

2

Put the plain and dark chocolates in a heatproof bowl and fit over a saucepan of simmering water (the bowl must not come in contact with the water). Let the chocolate melt.

3

Mix the ground cloves and cream in a bowl. Remove the chocolate from the heat and gently stir the clove cream into the melted chocolate – do not beat. Pour the mixture into the lined container, smooth with a palette knife, and chill until set.

4

When set, use the edges of the clingfilm to lift the chocolate slab from the container. Invert onto a wooden board and peel away the clingfilm. Bring to room temperature, then slice into cubes. Dust with cocoa, then serve with the berries.

600 g plain chocolate, broken into pieces

200 g dark cooking chocolate (70 per cent cocoa solids), broken into pieces

12 cloves, finely ground

750 ml double cream

unsweetened cocoa powder, for dusting

2–4 punnets golden raspberries or other berries, about 250 g in total

Makes about 36

Variations:

Serve sliced fresh figs, candied oranges or vanilla-poached pears instead of berries.
Raisins soaked in orange liqueur or orange flower water can be stirred into the chocolate mixture before it sets.

Summer pudding toast

Traditional English summer pudding, made from melted berries and juice-soaked bread, is delicious, but needs planning, to give it time to saturate and set. This combination of berry juices and strawberries on toast is an instant version – though the fruit mixture will still benefit from being left for a few hours if you have time. It looks just as elegant as the original.

4 punnets mixed berries, such as redcurrants, raspberries, blueberries and blackberries, about 500 g

125 g sugar

185 g strawberries, stems removed and halved

4 slices brioche or white bread

butter, for spreading

To serve:

wild strawberries (optional)

mint leaves

icing sugar, for dusting

thick double cream

Serves 4

1

Pick over the punnets of fruit, removing any stems or leaves. Put the berries in a saucepan with 60 ml water and the sugar. Bring to the boil, then reduce the heat and simmer gently for about 8 minutes.

2

Put the halved strawberries in a bowl and press the cooked fruit syrup through a non-metal sieve over the strawberries. Let stand for at least 30 minutes, then chill. Alternatively, leave overnight in the refrigerator.

3

When ready to serve, toast the brioche or bread, spread with butter and spoon the fruit syrup over each slice. Arrange the glazed strawberries over the tops, surround with wild strawberries, if using, and sugar-dusted mint leaves. Serve the cream separately.

Variations:

You needn't sieve the fruit, just pile it all on toast, top with thick cream and serve.
Try using warmed doughnuts instead of toast.
Serve the berry juice and strawberry mixture with vanilla ice-cream.

Blueberry cheesecake

Yes, there's a pastry to make, but it's so easy, and rolling it straight onto the tin stops it tearing. Easy to make and light to eat: the filling is virtually fat free and the pastry base is so thin you can have seconds without worrying about calories. The base and filling hold up well if you want to make it in advance – add the fresh fruit just before serving.

300 g blueberries or bilberries

mint leaves

icing sugar, for dusting

double cream, to serve (optional)

Pastry base:

60 g caster sugar

125 g unsalted butter, softened

1 egg yolk

1 teaspoon grated lemon zest

185 g plain flour, sifted

Cheesecake filling:

375 g low-fat soft cheese,
such as Quark

4 eggs, yolks and whites separated

1 teaspoon grated lemon zest

125 g caster sugar

1 tablespoon plain flour

Serves 6–8

1

Butter a 20 cm springform tin and base-line with greaseproof paper.

2

To prepare the pastry base mix the sugar, butter, egg yolk and lemon zest in a bowl. Add the flour and work to a smooth dough. If it is too sticky, dust with flour, then work in. Chill for 20 minutes.

3

Put the base of the springform tin on the work surface and roll out the pastry on top to approximately 5 mm thickness. Trim around the base with a knife and discard the excess pastry. Assemble the tin and bake in a preheated oven at 150ºC (300ºF) Gas 2 for 20 minutes until half cooked. Let cool. Reduce the oven heat to 140ºC (275ºF) Gas 1.

4

To make the cheesecake filling, mix the cheese in a bowl with the egg yolks and lemon zest. Beat the egg whites until stiff, then gradually beat in the sugar and flour. Fold the egg white mixture into the cheese mixture and spoon over the part-cooked pastry base in the tin. Sprinkle with 2 tablespoons of the berries and bake on the middle shelf of the oven for about 1 hour or until firm to the touch. Let cool.

5

To serve, top with a tumbling pile of the remaining fruit, scatter with a few mint leaves, dust with icing sugar and serve with cream, if using.

Lemongrass yoghurt rice
with crushed raspberries

Mix and match the refreshing lemongrass yoghurt rice with the sweet crushed fruit as you go – or you could even spoon the berries and juice into the bowls first and cover with the rice, then dig deep for the berries as you eat.

250 g raspberries

120 g caster sugar

1 tablespoon lemon juice

115 g pudding rice, washed

4 stalks lemongrass, trimmed and smashed open

700 ml milk

440 g creamy yoghurt

Serves 4

1

Put half the raspberries in a saucepan and stir in half the sugar and 1 tablespoon water. Bring to the boil, then reduce the heat and simmer until the fruit is soft. Push the fruit and juice through a non-metal sieve into a bowl, discarding the pips. Stir in the lemon juice, then add the remaining raspberries to the purée, crush lightly and let cool.

2

Put the rice, lemongrass, milk and the remaining caster sugar into a saucepan, bring to the boil, stir well, reduce the heat and simmer for 30 minutes. Let cool, then discard the lemongrass.

3

Stir the yoghurt into the lemongrass rice, then divide between 4 bowls and serve with small bowls of crushed raspberries.

Variations:

Flavour the rice with a split vanilla pod rather than lemongrass and serve with a purée of mixed berries.
Serve the raspberries with Greek yoghurt and honey, scattered with slivers of toasted almonds.

79

index